First World War
and Army of Occupation
War Diary
France, Belgium and Germany

14 DIVISION
Divisional Troops
224 Machine Gun Company
12 November 1917 - 28 February 1918

WO95/1890/3

The Naval & Military Press Ltd
www.nmarchive.com
Published in association with The National Archives

Published by

The Naval & Military Press Ltd

Unit 10 Ridgewood Industrial Park,

Uckfield, East Sussex,

TN22 5QE England

Tel: +44 (0) 1825 749494

www.naval-military-press.com

www.nmarchive.com

This diary has been reprinted in facsimile from the original. Any imperfections are inevitably reproduced and the quality may fall short of modern type and cartographic standards.

© **Crown Copyright**
Images reproduced by permission of The National Archives, London, England, 2015.

Contents

Document type	Place/Title	Date From	Date To
Heading	WO95/1890/3		
Heading	14 Div Troops 224 Machine Gun Coy 1917 Nov-1918 Feb		
War Diary	Southampton	12/11/1917	12/11/1917
War Diary	La Havre	13/11/1917	13/11/1917
War Diary	No 1 Rest Camp Section B. La Havre	14/11/1917	15/11/1917
War Diary	Wizernes	16/11/1917	16/11/1917
War Diary	Val D'Acquin	17/11/1917	03/12/1917
War Diary	Wizernes	03/12/1917	03/12/1917
War Diary	Vlamertinghe	03/12/1917	03/12/1917
War Diary	Brandhoek	03/12/1917	15/12/1917
War Diary	St Jean	16/12/1917	28/12/1917
War Diary	Westbecourt	29/12/1917	04/01/1918
War Diary	Morcourt	05/01/1918	28/02/1918

WO 95/1890 (3)   WO 95/1890 (3)

14 DIV TROOPS

224 MACHINE GUN COY

1917 NOV — 1918 FEB

Page 1.

224 Machine Gun Coy.

WAR DIARY
INTELLIGENCE SUMMARY.
(Erase heading not required.)

Army Form C. 2118.

Instructions regarding War Diaries and Intelligence Summaries are contained in F. S. Regs., Part II. and the Staff Manual respectively. Title pages will be prepared in manuscript.

Place	Date	Hour	Summary of Events and Information	Remarks and references to Appendices
Southampton.	12.11.17	9.0 A.M.	Arrival.	
do	12.11.17	7.30 P.M.	Departure 7.30 P.M. in 2 Parties.	
Le Havre	13.11.17	5.0 A.M.	Arrival 1st Party on "Prince George". Disembarked at 9.30 A.M. and marched to No.1 Rest Camp. Section B. arrival 10.30 A.M.	
do	13.11.17	3. P.M.	Arrival 2nd Party on "Viviana". Disembarked at 8.0 A.M. and marched to No.1 Rest Camp. Section B. arrival 6.0 P.M.	
No.1 Rest Camp	13.11.17		1.O.R. admitted to Hospital.	
Section B. La Havre	14.11.17		State of Camp. 1 Mule admitted Hospital.	
do	15.11.17	5.0 P.M.	Marched off, and entrained at Pond 3. at 9.3 P.M.	
Wizernes	16.11.17	8.30 A.M.	Arrival. Detrained and marched to Val d'Acquin and joined the 14th Division	
Val d'Acquin	17.11.17	3.30 A.M.	Arrival and Billeted.	
do	18.11.17		Church Parade. 1.O.R. admitted to Hospital.	
do	19.11.17		Programme of work carried out. Cleaning Gear, Guns etc.	
do	20.11.17		do.	Inspections. Infantry Drill. Infantry Drill and P.T. J.D. and R.T. Anti-Aircraft Instruction. Cleaning Guns, Gear & Wagons. Elementary Drill. I.A. Scouring use of Ground. Action from Limbers.
do	21.11.17		Football match with 143rd M.G. Coy. Result, drawn 1-1. Owing to Rain. Route march Cancelled.	Cleaning Gunscks. Cleaning Equipment. Lectured on "How to keep Guns firing in frosty weather" "Care of feet"
do	22.11.17		4 Officers and N.C.O's proceeded to No.9 Aircraft Supply Depot for instruction in judging height of Aeroplanes. Machine Guns placed at disposal for aiming practice. Remainder of Company carried out Programme of work.	Infantry Drill and P.T. Mechanism. Gun Drill Action Limber Drill. Extended Order Drill with Guns. (Battn Formation). Inspection of Box Respirators.
			Football match with A.S.C. Result A.S.C.3. 224 M.G.C.O.	

D. D. & L., London, E.C. (A501). Wt. W1771/M2031 750,000 5/17 Sch. 52 Forms. C2-0/14

Page 2.

WAR DIARY

INTELLIGENCE SUMMARY.

(Erase heading not required.)

224 Machine Gun Coy Army Form C. 2118.

Instructions regarding War Diaries and Intelligence Summaries are contained in F. S. Regs., Part II. and the Staff Manual respectively. Title pages will be prepared in manuscript.

Place	Date	Hour	Summary of Events and Information	Remarks and references to Appendices
Val d'Acquin	23.11.17		Programme of work carried out. Infantry Drill and P.T. Parade dabry. Gas.	Barrage Drill mechanism.
do	24.11.17		Programme of work carried out. Infantry Drill and P.T. I.A. Gas. Range Finders Tested. Wagons cleaned and axles greased.	Barrage Drill sorting. Anti-aircraft Instruction. Ammunition checked and cleaned.
do	25.11.17		Church Parade.	
do	26.11.17		Route March. Combining V.T. and I.D.	
do	27.11.17		Tactical Scheme cancelled, owing to inclement weather.	
do	28.11.17		Tactical Scheme. (Consolidation of Objective Semi-open warfare). Vicinity Val d'Acquin. I.A. mechanism carried on in billets.	
do	29.11.17		Company paraded for Bathe, and Divisional Baths Acquin. Wagons cleaned and Gun Gear checked. Emergency Rations issued. 2 Mules admitted Hospital. Rugby Match with 42nd M.G. Coy. Result 224th M.G. Coy. 7pts. 42nd M.G. Coy 6pts.	
do	30.11.17		Programme of work carried out. P.T. Demonstration of M.G. defence of line, Co-operation, Commencation and Pepper. Barrage Drill.	

W.G. [signature] Capt.
O.C. No 224 M.G. COY.

Army Form C. 2118.

244 Machine Gun Company

WAR DIARY
or
INTELLIGENCE SUMMARY.
(Erase heading not required.)

Instructions regarding War Diaries and Intelligence Summaries are contained in F. S. Regs., Part II. and the Staff Manual respectively. Title pages will be prepared in manuscript.

Place	Date	Hour	Summary of Events and Information	Remarks and references to Appendices
Val d'Acqui	1/12/17		Company paraded for cleaning up camp, packing wagons etc	
do	2/12/17	8.30 AM	Transport moved off. Formed K.3 with Pde Columns of Indauques, and marched to Chevingelle area	
do	2/12/17	1.0 PM	Inflammatory instructions to troops arrangements for billeting	
do	3/12/17		Company paraded for inspection at 9.30 AM. Tracking of Orders. 1 O.R. admitted to Hospital	
do	3/12/17	4.0 PM	Officers and 6 O.R. with Cooks, Carts, and Water cart, marched off	
do	3/12/17	5.15 AM	Remainder of Company marched off	
Ooys-onel	3/12/17	8.0 AM	Arrival and entrained	
do	3/12/17	9.30 AM	Detrained	
Vlamertinghe	3/12/17	10.5 AM	Arrival. Detrained and marched off	
Brandhoek	3/12/17	12.0	Arrival and billeted C/o 6.9.C.	
	3/12/17	2.0 PM	Transport moved off with 43 Inf.Bde Column from Vlamerghe to Broadhock. Co.bq.P. arrived 12.30 PM	
Brandhoek	4/12/17		Company installed in Gorbetown. Fit and Gun cleaning. 1 OR admitted to Hospital. 1 OR evacuated from	
			Hospital, and with the cur. Ascendale Ridge (about 3/4 mile).	
			40 Men with Runner Ag. 23rd & /43rd 1/4	
			40 Men in Support	
			40 at Rum Reserve	
			M.T. 40 Cooks Reserve	
do	5/12/17		Cleaning Guns, Ammunition, Wagons etc. Fed grained. 2 OR admitted to Hospital	
do	6/12/17		1 O.R. evacuated to Base underage.	
			1 OR proceeded to Corps on a Machine Gun Course to extend over form at the MG School	
			Fed. Inspection. Trench Feet Orill.	
			Physical Training. Lecture by Section Officers on the line	
			2 O.R. admitted to Hospital	
do	7/12/17		Fed. Inspection and Trench Feet Oriel.	
			Physical Training	
			Gun cleaning.	
			1 OR admitted to Hospital. 2 OR discharged Hospital.	

Army Form C. 2118.

224 Trench Gun Company

WAR DIARY
or
INTELLIGENCE SUMMARY.
(Erase heading not required.)

Instructions regarding War Diaries and Intelligence Summaries are contained in F. S. Regs., Part II. and the Staff Manual respectively. Title pages will be prepared in manuscript.

Place	Date	Hour	Summary of Events and Information	Remarks and references to Appendices
France	8.12.17		Post Inspection and Opened Feel Strills. Physical Training. Cleaning Guns, Bags etc. Barrage ordered to Westhoek Ridge at B.N.W. C.28.6 and to harass deep Camps at H.Q.c., Draaibank Tank at C.27.d. Transfer Farm Barrage to be on Fresh Barrel. At 2.10 PM 14 Guns Teamed on 6" Gun provided by Sedrow at 20 minutes intervals and recovered at 2" H.R.O.R. on R.Q. Gun. Rebel carried at 7.0 P.M. Casualties 1 O.R. slightly wounded Guns cleaning up on Pack mules to Waterloo Dump. No.4 28. D.9.d. Recce reconnoitred. 2 Guns of No. 4 M.G. Coy attached under the Command of 224 M.G. Coy. Total 14 Guns. Barrage position at D.5.d. 45 to 6. D.10.6. 85.85 pillboxes. Pakenhams (as field) Kap of Belgian Shed A.B. Barrage divided into 2 Platoons A and B, Platoon A Battery 8 Guns "B" Battery 6 Guns Ref. No. 8 at about W.25.a.7.6 & V.24.d 65.25 Target 13 "A" Battery V.24.a 65.35, V.24.d. 50.30 Coy HQ Headquarters at D.10.c.5.6 25. Personnel + transport. "B" Battery 2 Guns Coy Reserve at brick D.9.c.5.6 Pontoon under 2nd Bdgade at the Coc. Brigade Headquarters factor Pakenhams Ridge N25c.9.3 & V2.9 a.5.6 These brigade come from Pr. support line. 4 are shut at at back of mule Cel. Lieut. R.E. Rawlison and B. In C. B. recounted Casualty 1 Cpl. killed. 3 O.R. wounded Lieut Rawlison in gen. command of the Trench mortars. Hence a Section in gen. Command of the line at sector proposed at that 3 Guns in Cox Res. Mustlaw 3,000 rounds S.A.A. in Reserve during the night and day. Ammunition expended Nil. Casualties Nil.	
	9.12.17		Holding party heavy during the night and day. Ammunition expended Nil. Casualties Nil. 1 OR admitted to Hospital. 1 OR discharged hospital.	
	10.12.17		Section form at Shelling. Quiet day. Corps. The Guns Trench up to 6.30 dropped S.A.A. ours. Ammunition expended Nil. 1 OR admitted Sick.	
	12.12.17		Weather normal. Shelling not quite so intense. Gun Company relief carried out and completed by 4:0 P.M. Casualties Nil. Ammunition expended. Nil.	
	13.12.17		4 Lieut W.H.R. Grover and 3 O.R. proceeded to Tern Aerodrome to Anti-Aircraft Gunnery Course. Weather normal, Shelling very much decreased. Representatives to Brigade gave Gun Positions in Corps Reserve line. Ammunition expended Nil. Casualties Nil.	
			Orders received for 2nd Lieut A.R. Downey to proceed to England to undergo Medical Board in December 1, 1917. Authority A.D.140, 12 Dec. Precious Nothing to report.	

A.2092 W. 11125 9/M1293 750,000. 1/17. D.D & I Ltd. Forms/C2118/14.

Army Form C. 2118.

WAR DIARY
or
INTELLIGENCE SUMMARY.

(Erase heading not required.)

224 Machine Gun Company

Instructions regarding War Diaries and Intelligence Summaries are contained in F. S. Regs., Part II. and the Staff Manual respectively. Title pages will be prepared in manuscript.

Place	Date	Hour	Summary of Events and Information	Remarks and references to Appendices
	14.10.17		Situation found exceedingly quiet. Following fresh dispositions in Corps Reserve Line. 1st & 2nd Section. 1st O.O.0.15.60 3rd O.O.0.15.65. Three packers give good field of fire along the Corps Reserve in the Armentières Sector. 2 in & O of this Company reconnoitred. During the night enemy field Corps Reserve results 2 guns at Roved covered by platoon of shell and damaged beyond repair. Orders received that this M.G. Coy will take over on the morning of the 15th. Relieve of relief arranged between Company Commandos concerned.	
	15.10.17		At 7.0 A.M. Guides from all Gun Positions that 12 M.G. Coy at Wakeheof Swamp D.9.c. Gun teams Roved to Relief Camp independently. Relief complete by 9.30 A.M. Relief Camp at Knettje handed over to 41 M.G. Coy at 10.0 A.M. and company taken over Camp at Pecan D.27.b. 0.6 a.m. got into Bivouac Palace. Casualties 1 O.R. wounded	
Pecan	16.10.17		2 O.R. returned to Hospital Company paraded for cleaning guns, Gear and Wagons and checking same. 1 O.R. evacuated sick	
do	17.10.17		Company paraded for Inspection of Box Respirators, P.H. Helmets, Gas Curtains, Post Mortem Drill Cleaning of Gun Gear etc. promoted. 2 O.R. administratively reported sick or get Orders received from Division for 3 Guns to proceed to Horsea Road River to Corps Reserve Line	
do	18.10.17		3 Gun Guns proceeded from Ordnance Company paraded for Rifle Inspection. Direct Gas Drill. Returns received of Surplus of Section Officers. Medical orders for Ammunition Column. Full one Rifles of establishment. Company Inspected by Inspector Gen. Inspector Genl Inspection	
do	19.10.17		Arrived in Camp 23 pm Gun Orders received. No 1 Company with relieve no 2 M.G. Coy 29/10/19. Officers at Divisional School on return. M.G. Strng of Pt 21. Arrangements made for No 2 M.G. Coy regarding relief Guns and Ammo etc up D.Ct. Upon arrival and all are attached to Company for this turn of duty as the two Sectors Gun and only get ready Bolt Lines Ammunition Bundles Also Packs and Saving sight on approach 1 O.R. admitted Hospital and Evacuated.	

WAR DIARY or INTELLIGENCE SUMMARY

Army Form C. 2118.

224 Machine Gun Company

(Erase heading not required.)

Instructions regarding War Diaries and Intelligence Summaries are contained in F. S. Regs., Part II. and the Staff Manual respectively. Title pages will be prepared in manuscript.

Place	Date	Hour	Summary of Events and Information	Remarks and references to Appendices
	31.7.17		Company moves off by Sections at 5.10 P.M. Guides are met at Waterloo Bridge Sheet 28 N.W. Patricia House D.9.d.9.9. Relief complete at 8.50 P.M. Dispositions of Guns as follows: "A" Battery 8 Guns D.11.c.9.0.9 — "B" Battery 4 Guns D.5.d.75.10. 1st reaction S.O.S. lines to bring N.Q. Barrage from V.24.b.5.3 — Veg a.6.2 — W.25.a.55.55. 2 Guns at V.6.3.2. 2 Guns at full cal at Kerk D.9.a.5.6. 1 Gun at Wurst farm D.8.a.0.1. The last 3 Guns swing on this Schem line. Battery received that the two batteries in barrage work are to be moved as the Bosche is outside the Divisional area. Instructions are to act as follows. "A" battery 8 guns at D.4.b.45.05. "B" Battery 8 guns at D.4.b.3.12 Reaction in that direction quiet and at 11 O.A.M. orders issued for "B" Battery 4 guns, and "A" Battery 2 Guns to move to new positions, the remainder of the Guns taking over the whole target during the move. 2 Gs to Park together until the Guns as usual at D.4.b.6 formed into "B" Battery and placed in position with S.O.S lines at V.24.a.4.5. M.G.O.S. remainder of "A" Battery switches back onto the target. Large pa Bat in D.4.b is reached by B.H.Q. 3 Lieutenant on Lefts to reconnoitre "B" Battery. Relief complete and Company Camps in Day command of A.O.O 4.A.D. Starting Brigade. Casualties nil during the night 31st/1st. Harassing fire was carried out by 2 Guns "A" Battery at D.11.c into enemy tracks in squares V.24.a & 10. Ammunition expended 2800 rounds.	
		2.17	6 ears and 2 O.R. proceeded to Loshe Aerodrome. Four Prisoners with Gun Carriers & Amb. Car Bot Ramp & Prisoners to Bue and 83 O.R. endures received from D.H.Q.O. that emplacements are to be built at area trace in Losh Schem Line. 1 O.R. admitted Hospital.	
	1.8.17		Cat. Moore here reconnoitred and defensive emplacements sited and numbered as follows.	
			In H. Pat. {1st Gun D.9.c.9.5 firing due N. 10a " D.9.c.6.7 firing T bearing 55°	
			In H. Pat. {3rd Gun D.9.c.1.0 firing due N. 11a " D.8.d.9.5 firing T bearing 60°	
		1.5.12 1st	{5th & 6th Gun D.8.a.7.9 firing T bearing 10° 12a " D.7.b.4.2 firing T bearing 65°	

WAR DIARY or INTELLIGENCE SUMMARY

Army Form C. 2118.

224 Machine Gun Company

Place	Date	Hour	Summary of Events and Information	Remarks and references to Appendices
	22/12/17		Barbers 15 and 10A guns abreast in Barbers at Lock Barbers (2 guns abreast in section at Wurst Farm Barbers), No.2 and No.4 guns to be taken up by "X" guns 6 Company in position on Plateau of Craters. Weather clear and bright, enemy artillery fairly active. Hostile aircraft very active. Impossible to move guns by daylight to new Battery positions. However two guns were withdrawn from "A" Battery at dusk to new Barbers. Swing roll 22, 23. No harassing fire carried out by 2 guns "A" Battery on road to V.24.c. Ammunition expended 5000 rounds. 18,000 rounds SAA moved to new Battery position. At 5.0 PM S.O.S. went up (on rocket) heating into 2 Red and 2 White stars) "A" and "B" Batteries opened fire on S.O.S. lines for 15 minutes, when situation again became normal. Enemy did not attack in this sector. Casualties nil.	
	23/12/17		At night 22/23rd Pole relief takes place (I.O.O. H.M. Poll takes command of Coy. Emplacements dug and wired on the Corps line in Boesinghe Sector Wood. Heavy frost prevailed during the morning. Hostile artillery activity below normal. Enemy aircraft activity nil. Orders received for remaining 4 guns of "A" Battery to move from D.11.B to D.4.6. A consolidation for all personnel to have full box and SB. Battery Barbers now whole Target carried to "B" Battery. Move complete by 2.30 PM. Moved to the 1st cleaning and great enemy aircraft activity during afternoon. Impossible to layout lines for "A" Battery. 35,000 rounds SAA carried to new Battery position. During night 23/24 harassing fire carried out by No.5 and 8 "and 'B" Battery, target roadway W.25.a and W.19.c. Ammunition expended 5000 rounds. Casualties nil.	
	24/12/17		1 O.R. admitted, 1 O.R. discharged Hospital. 1 O.R. evacuated sick. 1 O.R. taken on strength. Arrangements made with O.C. support for H.Q. at Bellevue Dug in W.21.w. In the event of an enemy break through. Work on Battery work, wire & c. at his disposal for defence of Bellevue farm. Cookers etc. Lines laid out for "A" Battery. Target V.24.a.80.10 – W.25.a.55.55. 20,000 rounds SAA brought up to new Battery position. On night 24/25th harassing fire was carried out by No.7 and 8 and "B" Battery on target roadway V.24.d.50.30. Ammunition expended 4000 rounds. Casualties nil.	
	25/12/17		S.O.A.P. Sundri heavy shelling of Ziele ins spur in vicinity of Battery position for hours. Enemi shelled Krongsbout Redoy rather heavy. SAA brought up from dump 10,000 rounds. During day Battery positions were improved and shelter made for personnel and cook. Harassing fire was carried out by 2 guns "B" Battery in vicinity of V.24.d.50.30 and 4 guns "B" Battery in vicinity of V.24.d.50.30. Casualties. 1 O.R. accidentally wounded.	

Army Form C. 2118.

WAR DIARY
or
INTELLIGENCE SUMMARY.

224 Machine Gun Company

(Erase heading not required.)

Instructions regarding War Diaries and Intelligence Summaries are contained in F. S. Regs., Part II. and the Staff Manual respectively. Title pages will be prepared in manuscript.

Place	Date	Hour	Summary of Events and Information	Remarks and references to Appendices
Cattenach	2/12/17		O.C. 224 M.G. Coy. visited Company H.Q. and arrangements were made regarding relief of Company by 14th N.Cdn. and 2 Guns 25th M.G. Coy. during this time, on the line the ground had been in a very open and cultivated nature. Ground covered with show. Enemy artillery fairly active throughout the day. Considerable enemy aircraft activity from 11.0 A.M onwards. 6.0 P.M enemy shelled roads and tracks leading from ... train sent to Bellevue Cr. marching magazine relay. Field of arc cables and carriers all the number of Ros. plate being sited. Gun party relay in progress. Company withdrew and returned to 14th N.Cdn. Relay Company at 8.0 A.M. brought up. Company proceeded to detail Camp at Wares.	
	3/12/17		Company travelled at 1.10 P.M. for Westhercourt. ... with orders left the rear encampments at Wares.	
	4/12/17		Ck 10.0 A.M. Company proceeded to Mote Road to Westhercourt. Relief to 6 hrs and the Railway Convoys ... Railroad the convoy arrived to Rail Services Jonathan Rose Junction, and R.E. Company proceeded to Westhercourt. Rail Services arrived at 4.30 P.M. One of the Lorries found to be a pioneer around company arrived at Westhercourt the Region.	
Westhercourt	5/12/17		The next morning trunk came and part and the baggage sent was brought in. Company proceed for Foot Friction Spills. Equipment cleaned.	
do	6/12/17		Foot Friction Spills. Guns clean cleaned and checked. Wagons packed.	
do	7/12/17		Foot Friction Spills. Running and traveling Drills. Company inspected Full traveling Order. Kit Inspection. Sick Report. Sew ... as a ... checked to 4th Army Taxation School at ...	
			S.O. examined Hospital 10R discharge of hospital.	

J.C. No. 224 M.G. Coy.

Army Form C. 2118.
NO. 224 COY. M.G.C.

Frankish W.J.

Vol 3

WAR DIARY
or
INTELLIGENCE SUMMARY.
(Erase heading not required.)

224 Machine Gun Company

Instructions regarding War Diaries and Intelligence Summaries are contained in F. S. Regs., Part II. and the Staff Manual respectively. Title pages will be prepared in manuscript.

Place	Date	Hour	Summary of Events and Information	Remarks and references to Appendices
Wallecourt	1-1-18		Company paraded for bathing, bogged up. Lectures for morning. In the evening a concert was held which proved successful and a very enjoyable evening was spent. 2 O.R. evacuated sick.	
	2-1-18		Company paraded at 11.30 A.M. and marched to Sotteringham. Looks in a very bad condition. Arrived at 13.30 PM and billeted. 3 O.R. evacuated sick.	
	3-1-18		Lectures on Company Sections, backing, bogging etc. at 6 PM Company paraded to go to a bath in the huts at Flêtre/Trenchelham. Strong wind. Supplied at 7.15. On our train travel arrived at 9.30 P.M.	
	4-1-18		Company had road work on 3-30AM extensive and Company marched off at 10-30 AM to the canal and halted in the village. Also the van route march taken proved very welcome to the men coming to the heavy going and the Rogers condition of the roads. On col Anthony's suggestion was experienced in billets. Remained along with teams had to be boarded up and the turners with the back woods.	
Toutencourt	5-1-18		Company paraded for Foot Inspection Drill. Bathes thoroughly cleaned. 1 O.R. evacuated to an ad. Conv. Depot E.R.D at a. Course. 1 O.R. evacuated sick.	
	6-1-18		Foot Inspection Drill. Equipment cleaned.	
"	7-1-18		S.A. and Mechanism. Saddle Exercises. Long train renovation & programme cancelled.	
"	8-1-18		Gun Drill. Foot Drill. Personal Inspection. Lecture on Chevrolutions.	
	9-1-18		Company paraded for Battesis 1. 3 O.R. evacuated sick. Gun Drill and P.T. Extended Order & Location Mechanism. Avocation of Bathes.	
"	10-1-18		Gen. Sec'n. Lecture held between 1P.L and 1.30 Section. Rebelt Registration Zones, 1o3 Section Drills. Foot Section Drills. Gun Drill and P.T. Gun Drill Elementary. S.A. Mechanism. S.A. helmet. Gun Lateral and Field openings, 19 Gocke. Types of Control. 600 Reparators. S.N. helmet. Gun Lateral and Field openings, 19 Gocke.	

January 2.

224 Machine Gun Company

Army Form C. 2118.

WAR DIARY
or
INTELLIGENCE SUMMARY.
(Erase heading not required.)

Place	Date	Hour	Summary of Events and Information	Remarks and references to Appendices
Tincourt	10-1-18		Inter Section Football Match between Nos 2 and 4 Sections. Result No 2 Section Egoals No 4 Section 0.	
do	11-1-18		Foot Section Drill. Infantry Drill and P.T. Gun Drill advanced.	
			Packing and unpacking limbers including S.A.A. wagons. Lecture on spare Parts	
			L.O.R. taken on strength.	
do	12-1-18		Infantry Drill and P.T. Section Scheme and Kit Inspection.	
do	13-1-18		Church Parade.	
do	14-1-18		Football Match between 224 M.G.C. and B. Coy. Bedfordshire Light Infantry. Result B.L.I. 2 goals 224 M.G.C. nil	
			Foot Section Drill. Battery Position King or Rouge. Stoppages finish in Reapernam.	
			3 O.R. evacuated. 1 O.R. admitted Hospital	
do	15-1-18		Foot Section Drill. Infantry Drill. One horse from Wagon	
			Section from Park and Loading Gun positions and ammunition supply.	
			Football match with 11th Battalion Kings Liverpools in the 1st round for the Divisional Cup.	
			Result 11th Battn Kings Liverpools 8 goals 224 MGC, nil	
do	16-1-18		Foot Section Drill. Infantry Drill. Asst in Gun Bunkers	
			Forage Fuel and Forage. Lecture on Indirect Fire	
do	17-1-18		Visited to Team and Observation Posts was cancelled	
do	18-1-18		Foot Section Drill. I.R. Competition. Division A.R. Carried on in Billets	
			Park to send of about 65 Rifles. Whistle with A.R. of Company as a "Rifle" from Limbers	
			One driver Adventures Limbers are then was Ridded by a Mule in the face, and was admitted to Hospital	
			L.O.R. Taken on strength. 1 O.R. proceeded to U.R. on leave.	
do	19-1-18		Foot Section Drill. Infantry Drill. Gun Stoppages Kit Inspection	
			Football match with Division Light Infantry. Result 224 M.G.C. 3 goals D.L.I. 1 goal	
do	20-1-18		Church Parade. L.O.R. discharged Hospital	
do	21-1-18		Full turning Order Inspection. Guns Gear Wagons checked and cleaned	
			Wagon tracks on "The Down" for training. H. U.F. admitted Hospital. 1 O.R. evacuated. 1 O.R. proceeded on leave to U.K.	

WAR DIARY or INTELLIGENCE SUMMARY

Army Form C. 2118.

(Erase heading not required.)

124th Machine Gun Company

Place	Date	Hour	Summary of Events and Information	Remarks and references to Appendices
Janvan 3	22-1-18		Company paraded at 8.30 A.M. to march to Frangest en-partang arrived at 1-15 P.M and billeted. Lieut ? W Walding left at 8.0 A.M to make arrangements for billeting. 1 Mule admitted to 26th Mobile Veterinary Section. 4 O.R. evacuated sick.	
	23-1-18		Company moved off at 7.45 A.M from Frangest en-partaine to march to Labourene and arrived at 11-50 A.M and billeted	
	24-1-18		Company paraded at 7.45 A.M for march from Labourene to Dalet and arrived at Dalet at 1-30 P.M and billeted	
	25-1-18		Company moved off at 11-30 A.M from Dalet and arrived at Cuiscard at 3-45 P.M and billeted.	
	26-1-18		Company moves from Cuiscard to Sussy into Sellets. Capt ? & Bar and Lieut ? W Walding proceeded to Brigade Headquarters at Morlecourt from where they proceeded at 5.0 P.M in the event to reconnoitre the line to be taken over from the French. Reconnaisance continued at 1.0 P.M. Pin Gun teams arrive and carry on ammunition to M.G emplacements. No transport in the line for the night. 1 O.R. proceeded to Base for his proceeding to Egypt. 1 O.R. taken in strength. 1 O.R. admitted to Hospital. Authority 116th Division M/51/249	
	28-1-18		The Company relieved the Gens of the M.G Company of 41st Div a/13. By Rets relief Car.ed at 11.0 P.M Dispositions Rel was Raven Street 630 M.W. Dugouts H 12 d 1.8 1 Emerging NE H 12 d 3.0 1 " Sand 4ming 110° H 12 d 8.4 1 " " " 150° H 12 d 8.8 1 " " " 100° Hus 4 Mus Gun Battery and are manned by No1 Section 1 Company R.R.O.L. Dugouts in reach of Hess Gard. Section Hqst H.12 d 2.2	

Army Form C. 2118

No. 224 COY. M.G.C.

WAR DIARY
or
INTELLIGENCE SUMMARY.

(Erase heading not required.)

January 4

224 Machine Gun Company

Instructions regarding War Diaries and Intelligence Summaries are contained in F. S. Regs., Part II. and the Staff Manual respectively. Title pages will be prepared in manuscript.

Place	Date	Hour	Summary of Events and Information	Remarks and references to Appendices
	16.1.18		H. 18. c. 1. 6 Gun firing in True bearing 130° H. 18.o.1.5 " " " " " 165° H. 23.6.8.8. " " " " " 100° Was Gun manned by No. 5 section section 1 D at H. 18.o.1.5 H.24.c.4.4 and H.24.c.8.4 Guns found down taken to N. of Bois-de-Ree True bearing about 65° H.20.a.4. 9pm Found in True bearing 140° Above broken train by No 2 section. Section A.Q at H.24.c.1.6 Company HQ situated Wolart Farm H.17.d.4.1 Remainder of Company and transport bivac at Senin 1 O.R. taken to hospital	

	20.1.18		Section moved to Eouve Bivouacs. Block Gun Commander withdrawing M.G's W.G. Wood and 25 Co to C.C from advance South Wight. Wire erected out in improving entrenchments and fillers in roadway undertaken. Ammunition and Bombs carried up great distance from No.3 road to Eugnatte Farm at H.4.d. out 3 guns at about H.2.4.a HQ moved to new position at H.24.a.2.5 where a better field of fire obtained in roads to advance.
			Afternoon forming in the Ghos, snow falling slight. Observations from Doisons Road East of
			noticed in Ambulances in Fields, Bugris & Crown - Zenan Aeroplane with two E.g Zeppelins.
			carried up 4 Companion's N° 1 Sect. to No.1 Aeroplanes. This Aeroplane observed day as & various
			Service at 4.55 a 4.8
			         4.55 a 45 80
			         H. 22 c 56
			         4.22 c 4 8
			         4.23 c 48
			         4.21 d 36
			         4.21 d 44
			Saccour Soldier reported to Doctor.	

WAR DIARY
or
INTELLIGENCE SUMMARY

224 Machine Gun Company

January 1918

Place	Date	Hour	Summary of Events and Information	Remarks and references to Appendices
	2/1/18		1 O.R. taken on strength. 1 O.R. admitted to hospital. 1 Mule admitted to 26 Mobile Vet Section	
	3/1/18		Two indirect fire emplacements at H.8.C.9.4. also two at H.24.a.05.50. Alternative emplacements and Gun Carriers completed at all positions. Ammunition and Gun Carriers completed at all positions. Communications. Two baskets for waggons to carry gear are about 15 Kilos each.	

Alexander Lieut
for O.C. No. 224 M.G. COY.

Army Form C. 2118.

WAR DIARY
or
INTELLIGENCE SUMMARY.
(Erase heading not required.)

224 Machine Gun Company

Instructions regarding War Diaries and Intelligence Summaries are contained in F. S. Regs., Part II. and the Staff Manual respectively. Title pages will be prepared in manuscript.

February.

Place	Date	Hour	Summary of Events and Information	Remarks and references to Appendices
	1.2.18		To the line. Situation normal. Rifle activity slight. Enemy obtained direct hit on emplacement at H.16.c.1.5 but did no damage. General improvements made to emplacements, recesses etc. Casualties nil.	
	2.2.18		Front Line Guns at H.2.d. rearranged as follows:— Left Gun placed at H.2.d.1.9 firing on bearing 110°T. Right Gun at H.12.d.3.6 altered to fire on bearing 5°T. to Cross fire with Gun of 2nd N.Z.M.G.Coy. firing from H.6.C.8.3. During the night an unknown Company relief was carried out and completed by 11.0.P.M. Relieved personnel returned to Transport Lines at Suzu. Situation quiet. Casualties nil. Enemy aircraft active throughout the day. All Enemy Aeroplanes which crossed our lines flying at a low altitude were engaged by fire. 1 O.R. admitted Hospital. 1 O.R. taken on strength.	
	3.2.18		Alternative emplacements made to all front line positions. A.A. emplacements made as follows:— H.16.c.1.6 (1 gun) H.23.b.8.8 (1 gun) H.25.b.95.35 (2 guns). Enemy activity slight. Hostile aircraft active throughout the day. Situation normal. Indirect harassing fire carried out by 2 Guns from H.23.b.0.4 on trenches of enemy front line at I.14 Central and Cross roads at I.8.C.5.4. Ammunition expended 3000 rounds. Casualties Nil. All enemy aeroplanes which crossed our lines flying at a low altitude were engaged by fire.	
	4.2.18		Force Rokeskilling in neighbourhood of front line Guns. No.11330 Pte Hanna J. wounded in the hand. Work carried on, generally improving emplacements, recesses, trenches etc. Artillery activity normal, seems to be carrying out a fair amount of registration in connection with aeroplane observation. Otherwise nothing to report. Casualties 1 O.R. wounded. Orders issued for teams to be practiced daily in bearing Coc Reservoirs. 6 Gun teams with Gun orders from Suzu for the purpose of occupying Benay line from N. of Benay to N. of Henecourt. Teams and Gun Crew accomodated at Benay for the night. All enemy aeroplanes which crossed our line flying at a low altitude were engaged by fire. 1 O.R. discharged Hospital. 1 Officer and 2 O.R. returned from Course at Pierrecourt.	

D. D. & L., London, E.C.
(A8001) Wt. W2771/M2031 750,000 5/17 Sch. 52 Forms/C2118/14

WAR DIARY
INTELLIGENCE SUMMARY

224 Machine Gun Company.
February.

Army Form C. 2118.

Place	Date	Hour	Summary of Events and Information	Remarks and references to Appendices
	5.2.18		Hostile aircraft very active; Raids have been engaged by 4 guns very heavily especially in afternoon. About 3.30 one enemy plane reported by Infantry to have been hit. Rounds expended on aircraft about 3,500. New battle emplacement made at H.8.c.0.8. Artillery activity slight. Situation normal. Casualties nil.	
	6.2.18		Hostile aircraft engaged between 3.30 and 4.30 P.M. Rounds expended 2,000. Artillery activity slight. Situation normal. Casualties 1 O.R. No.12721 Pte Bradrick G. wounded in left hand by H.E. Emplacement finished in Corps Defence Line. Ammunition and Tripods put in position. 1 O.R. returned from Course of Gunnery.	
	7.2.18		Situation normal. Casualties nil, nothing to report. Corps Defence Line reconnoitred with Brigadier 2/2nd Bde, and defensive positions discussed. 1 O.R. returned from leave. 1 O.R. admitted to Hospital.	
	8.2.18		Situation normal. Casualties nil. Nothing to report. Divn. Reg.l 8/9 1/4th Coy Reserve Line, 1 Sub Section of No.2 Section, 1 Sub Section of No.3 Section took over front line under Lt R E Savenkill. Front line No.1 Section on being relieved took over reserve line. 6 guns Rgt.13 guns under 2/Lt Douche. Left guns under 2/Lt B Skinner. Corps Line guns relieved by 6 teams from Transport. Camp at .... and returned to Subsy in relief. Relief complete at 11 O.P.M. Corps Defence line reconnoitred with Col M and 4/10th Brigade Commanding 1st Division M.G. Battn. and 8 defensive positions chosen. 1 O.R. discharged Hospital. 1 O.R. evacuated.	
	9.2.18		Between 3.0 and 4.0 A.M. enemy placed barrage in vicinity I.13.c after attempted raid on one of our posts. Barrage lasted about 15 minutes. Hostile aircraft engaged 9.40 A.M. - 500 rounds expended, otherwise situation normal. Casualties nil. New positions made in Corps Defence Line.	

Army Form C. 2118.

No. 224 COY. M.G.C.

3   Zetrward

WAR DIARY
224 Machine Gun Company.
INTELLIGENCE SUMMARY.

(Erase heading not required.)

Instructions regarding War Diaries and Intelligence / Summaries are contained in F. S. Regs., Part II. and the Staff Manual respectively. Title pages will be prepared in manuscript.

Place	Date	Hour	Summary of Events and Information	Remarks and references to Appendices
	9-2-18		As under, Tripods, ammunition and Bombs placed in each position and fields of fire marked.	
			No 1 position H.27.c.50.50 Firing along spur in H.28.a and b.	
			" 2 " H.27.b.50.55 " " down valley in H.28.d.2.0	
			" 3 " H.21.d.30.80 " " to H.28 Central	
			" 4 " H.21.d.50.90 " " towards H.22 Central.	
			" 5 " H.22.c.80.70 " " Along spur to H.28.C. Central	
			" 6 " H.22.a.25.55 " " N.E. of Rambar Wood	
			" 7 " H.22.a.55.75 " " down valley S.W. of Gouzy.	
			" 8 " H.16.c.4.1 " " Flanking cover N.E. of Rambar Wood.	
			Nos 3 and 4 Patrono are in new position and no guns placed here. 1 Officer and 2. O.R. proceeded on course to Douler Court. 1 O.R. evacuated. S.A.A. and Bombs carried up to Front Line Station. Situation normal. Casualties nil, nothing to report.	
	10.2.18		Two A.A. emplacements made at Benay in Corps Defence Line, to be manned during day by Corps Reserve Line Guns for A.A. work. Orders received from Division that 43rd and 43rd Bde are anxious to have a gun placed in Corps Defence Line somewhere rear H.27.a Central. Portion E. of London Wood at H.6.C.4.7. handed over to #21 M.G.Coy in order to release gun for new position. New Position between H.27.d.72.15 firing down valley in H.28 Central.	
	11-2-18		Nothing to Report. Casualties nil, Situation normal. Emplacement at H.27.d.72.15 Complete, and Report ammunition in place in position. 10,000 rounds S.A.A. Brought up to Benay Line, 10,000 to Front Line, and 10,000 to Coy. H.Q. All guns completed to 5000 rounds reserve.	
	12-2-18		Situation normal. Casualties nil. Mobile M.G. located at about I.7.c.9.4. This gun was very active firing on our trenches from H.18.6.8.5. to H.12.c.9.9. getting good bands of reverse in enfilade. 500 rounds fired by Front Line guns from firing positions on Enemy's forward positions, Enemy M.G's very active by stand to in the evening firing at our front line between points 90.P.H and 3.O.A.M.	Regd 12/2/18 M2

A.7052 Wt. W.1125 9/M.1293 750,000. 1/17. D. D. & L. Ltd. Forms/C2118/14

WAR DIARY

4 February — 224 Machine Gun Company

INTELLIGENCE SUMMARY:
(Erase heading not required)

Place	Date	Hour	Summary of Events and Information	Remarks and references to Appendices
	12.2.18		Indirect harassing fire carried out from special positions at H.18.c.8.7, H.23.b.95.30 and H.23.b.95.40, on to enemy's positions at I.8.c.35.65, I.13.b.90.75 and I.7.a.50.10. Ammunition expended 7,000 rounds. During night 12/13th Gun teams were relieved as follows:— Front line the 2 Section. Reserve line No 1 Section. Corps line No.3 Section. Transport Camp, Sussex. Hot Section. 1.O.R. proceeded in course to III Corps Goodalet, Beaumont-en-Bene. 1.O.R. evacuated.	
	13.2.18		Situation normal, fair amount of hostile MG activity during morning and afternoon. A hostile MG broke out yesterday was again very active during early morning. Lt. R.E. Davenhill moved his two Left hand guns down Claudie Alley & old abandoned front line at about H.12.b.7.4 and each gun fired a belt at suspected block of hostile MG. Whereat was fired. Hostile MG then ceased fire and gave no trouble afterwards. During afternoon hostile MG showed great activity from enemy's trenches in I.7.d and I.13.b. The guns mentioned above were moved to improve positions at H.12.b.7.4 and H.12.d.9.4 from which positions 6,000 rounds were fired into enemy trenches in above mentioned vicinity which quietened the enemy MG activity. Otherwise nothing to report. Casualties nil. Orders issued for inter-Company relief for night of 14th:— No.3 Section to front line " 4 " , Reserve line No.1 " , Corps line No.2 " , Transport Camp, Sussex. From 11th onwards Meteorological reports received direct from 2nd Army to M.G. Companies. 1.O.R. admitted Hospital.	

Army Form C. 2118.

WAR DIARY

224 Machine Gun Company

INTELLIGENCE SUMMARY.

(Erase heading not required.)

Instructions regarding War Diaries and Intelligence Summaries are contained in F. S. Regs., Part II. and the Staff Manual respectively. Title pages will be prepared in manuscript.

Place	Date	Hour	Summary of Events and Information	Remarks and references to Appendices
	14.2.18		During day front line guns fired about 1500 rounds from Keeping Positions on 16 enemy reached in vicinity of I.9.b. Enemy M.G's had been very active from his neighbourhood and by a like amount retaliation. Their activity ceased. At night 14/15th inter-coy relief took place. No 3 Section front line under 2/Lt Green. No 4 Section Reserve line under 2/Lt Menzies and 2/Lt Dowdle. No 1 Section Coys Line under Lt Walding. No 2 Section Transport. Guns & ammunition Transport Gun Group. Situation normal. Casualties nil.	
	15.2.18		10 O.R. evacuated to Hospital. Guns in forward field numbered as follows :— H.18.C.60.60 — B.1 gun H.18.C.80.65 — B.2 gun H.12.a.30.60 — B.3 gun H.12.a.05.85 — B.4 gun Reserve line as follows :— H.24.c.95.45 — B.5 gun H.24.a.10.40 — B.6 gun H.24.a.10.45 — B.7 gun H.23.B.95.80 — B.8 gun H.18.C.80.80 — B.9 gun H.17.B.05.20 — B.10 gun B.5 position occupied by gun from H.24.c.40.25. B.8 position on Rue Gorre occupied by Gun which was at H.23.B.85.80. B.9.10 moved into above position from H.17.a.95.98. During day the following Reserve Guns were called into direct fire on enemy front line ready to open fire in case of S.O.S. as follows :— B.6 on G.I.9.a.85.60 B.7 .. I.7.a.60.10 B.8 .. I.13.B.40.87 B.9 .. I.13.G.75.80 B.10 .. I.14.a.50.50.	

Army Form C. 2118.

224 Machine Gun Company.

WAR DIARY
or
INTELLIGENCE SUMMARY.
(Erase heading not required.)

Instructions regarding War Diaries and Intelligence Summaries are contained in F. S. Regs., Part II. and the Staff Manual respectively. Title pages will be prepared in manuscript.

6. February.

Place	Date	Hour	Summary of Events and Information	Remarks and references to Appendices
	15-2-18		Emplacements made at 3 reserve positions. During day 1000 rounds expended on S.O.S. At 3-30 p.m. our Corps line Lewis gun carried out at S.O.S. on Hamelincourt. During day our front line guns fired 1500 rounds from improved positions on enemy movement at about I.13.6 and I.8.c. Situation normal. Casualties nil. 1 O.R. proceeded to Camieres on Course. 1 O.R. taken on strength.	
	16-2-18		E.A. fairly active during morning flying high. 1250 rounds fired from front line during day on I.13.6 and I.8.c. Otherwise nothing to report. Situation normal. Casualties nil. 4 O.R. taken on Strength. 1 O.R. admitted Hospital. 2 O.R. evacuated. 1 O.R. returned from Course at III Corps Gas School.	
	17-2-18		1400 rounds fired from front line on enemy trenches at I.14.a and I.13.c. Enemy aircraft engaged during day. Situation normal. Casualties nil. 4 O.R. taken on strength. 1 O.R. admitted Hospital. 1 O.R. evacuated. 1 O.R. discharged Hospital.	
	18-2-18		1,200 rounds expended from front line on to enemy trenches and movement. About 4-30 A.M. enemy put up 3 red rockets, resultant action barrage placed in vicinity of Mory. Otherwise nothing further to report. Situation normal. Casualties nil. 2 O.R. taken on strength.	
	19-2-18		1,500 rounds expended from front line into I.13.6 and I.y.d. Otherwise nothing to report. Situation normal. Casualties nil. 4 O.R. taken on Strength. 1 O.R. admitted Hospital.	
	20-2-18		During day 1000 rounds expended on enemy movement from front line. During night inter-company relief carried out. No.1 Section front line under 2/Lt. Harvey, No.3 Section reserve line under Pt/Lt. Skinner and 2/Lt. Green, No.2 Section Corps line under Lt. R.E. Davenhill	

Army Form C. 2118.

224 Machine Gun Company

WAR DIARY
INTELLIGENCE SUMMARY.
(Erase heading not required.)

Instructions regarding War Diaries and Intelligence Summaries are contained in F. S. Regs., Part II. and the Staff Manual respectively. Title pages will be prepared in manuscript.

February

Place	Date	Hour	Summary of Events and Information	Remarks and references to Appendices
	10.2.18		15 rounds fired every ½ hour to keep rifles cool. Situation normal. Casualties Nil. 1 O.R. to Rew or Strength. 1 O.R. discharged Hospital.	
	21.2.18		100 rounds expended from front line on enemy bivouac opposite. Situation normal. Casualties nil. At request of Brigadier General Commanding 14th Bde. the 6 guns in reserve line are arranged to place an indirect fire Barrage in No Man's Land from I.7.d.20.70 to I.7.d.30.20 and from I.7.d.00.70.65 I.13.b.00.60 instead of being laid in enemy front line as heretofore. This Barrage is opened and is to be fired down in case of S.O.S. Situation normal. Casualties nil. 2/Lt. P.D. Taylor proceeded to join No. 46 Division for duty. Authority A.G.8010	
	22.2.18		1,200 rounds expended from front line firing bursts on to enemy front line in vicinity of I7.a and I7.b. All gun positions in Costa Lane advance made up to 1000 rounds S.A.A. reserve. All S.A.A. in this line are now complete for 1 dogged emplacement, reserves and alternative emplacements. A dump of 29,000 rounds S.A.A. made at Pen-an, near Section Headquarters. Application made 15 Bde. for reserve section to be placed in Rule Gun position in front and reserve lines have all been sandbagged, brushes rivetted and floor dragged, and alternative emplacements made. 200 Boxes filled for B1 and B2 guns Front line. Two positions about 40 X N of old positions ranged. 4.6.6.8.65 Field of fire same as before, work commenced to build emplacements. Shell Camp heavy from 6.w.f. to 11 a.m. 3rd & 2nd I.R. 1 I.R. admitted Hospital	
	23.2.18		1,200 rounds expended from front line firing bursts on enemy front line. B1 and B2 guns traversed to rear positions whilst Rene row were completed. Otherwise nothing to report. Situation normal. Casualties nil. 1 O.R. at the Hospital	
	24.2.18		Our Artillery were active throughout the day. ~~Enemy returned our fire~~ A.O.R. taken on Strength. 1 O.R. admitted Hospital. 1 O.R. discharged Hospital	

Army Form C. 2118.

WAR DIARY
INTELLIGENCE SUMMARY
(Erase heading not required.)

224 Machine Gun Company.

Instructions regarding War Diaries and Intelligence Summaries are contained in F. S. Regs., Part II. and the Staff Manual respectively. Title pages will be prepared in manuscript.

February

Place	Date	Hour	Summary of Events and Information	Remarks and references to Appendices
	24-2-18		Enemy Aircraft fairly active. One M/G engaged Hun. Enemy shelled Battlezone but Aerial Observation otherwise nothing to report. Situation normal. Casualties nil.	
	25-2-18		Ordersreceived to move Coy. H.Q. to Bde H.Q. 1000 Rounds expended from sniping position in front line on enemy trenches I.7.d. Otherwise nothing to report. Casualties nil. 1 O.R. proceeded on leave to U.K.	
	26-2-18		1,250 Rounds expended sniping from front line on enemy parties in I.3.c. Enemy Aircraft active, engaged by M/G's. Enemy shelled Area of Gunpits, Cross Roads and Wood also Corps Line at 6-15 P.M. During night Inter Coy Relief carried out. No 1 Section to Front thereunder Lieut. J.W. Waldron. No 2 Section to reserve line under Lt. H.E. Saunders and 2.W.H. Douche. No 3 Section Corpstine. No 3 Section to Camp at Gully Relief Complete at 10-30 p.m. Situation normal. Nothing to report. Casualties nil.	
	27-2-18		Detail Club moved from La Trotte Hutsto Gully. 10R Admitted Hospital. 10R Evacuated. Conference of In.C. Commanders with Bum In.C. Commander held at H.2 Bde H.Q. 2-30 P.M. Re discuss formation of New Battalion.	
	28-2-18		1.0 P.M. orders received that the Corps Defence Line this was done all teams attamo Stadiasat 1-30 P.M. Enemy Aircraft very active, also Arla. Teams in forward zone warned against Possible attack, otherwise situation normal. Casualties nil. 4/5 M.M.G Coy orderedup to Corpstine. 2 Guns placed in Beray under Command of this Company. No offensive action taken by the enemy. 1 O.R. proceeded on Cookery Course. 4 OR taken on Strength.	

A. Booker Lt.
O.C. No. 224 M.G. COY.

www.ingramcontent.com/pod-product-compliance
Lightning Source LLC
Chambersburg PA
CBHW081506160426
43193CB00014B/2604